D0660968

SHADOW ARCHITECT

BOOKS BY EMILY WARN

The Leaf Path
The Novice Insomniac
Shadow Architect

SHADOW ARCHITECT

EMILY WARN

Tycher Library
7900 Northaven Road
Dallas, TX 75230

COPPER CANYON PRESS

PORT TOWNSEND, WASHINGTON

Copyright 2008 by Emily Warn

All rights reserved

Printed in the United States of America

Cover art: Dennis Evans, *The Sounds of the Exiles* (2006), from the series *Trace Elements: 22 Kits of Creation*. Encaustic and mixed media on canvas, 48 x 48 inches.

Copper Canyon Press is in residence at Fort Worden State Park in Port Townsend, Washington, under the auspices of Centrum. Centrum is a gathering place for artists and creative thinkers from around the world, students of all ages and backgrounds, and audiences seeking extraordinary cultural enrichment.

LIBRARY OF CONGRESS CATALOGING-IN-PUBLICATION DATA
Warn, Emily.
  Shadow architect / Emily Warn.
    p. cm.
  ISBN 978-1-55659-277-5 (pbk. : alk. paper)
  1. Hebrew language—Alphabet—Poetry. 1. Title.

  PS3573.A763S53 2008
  811'.54—dc22

                                    2008004855

98765432 FIRST PRINTING

COPPER CANYON PRESS
Post Office Box 271
Port Townsend, Washington 98368
www.coppercanyonpress.org

ACKNOWLEDGMENTS

Thanks to the following journals, books, and newspapers where some of these poems first appeared: *Blackbird, The Forward, From the Fishhouse,* and *Long Journey: Contemporary Northwest Poets.*

   To stay attuned to the letters' Jewish religious meanings, I read and reread *The Alef-Beit: Jewish Thought Revealed through the Hebrew Letters,* by Rabbi Yitzchak Ginsburgh. To understand the thinking contained in that book from historical and scholarly perspectives, I read the many books on the Kabbalah by Gershom Scholem, its seminal Jewish scholar. To live the Jewish tradition, I studied Hebrew in Seattle with Rabbi Fern Feldman, who also helped me in researching Talmudic sources; I studied the Torah and Talmud with an inspired Jewish educator named Rivy Kletenik, also in Seattle; and I joined the congregation of a beloved rabbi named Tom Gutherz in Lynchburg, Virginia, when I lived there.

FOR DAJ OBERG AND DENNIS EVANS

CONTENTS

INSTRUCTION FOR LIGHTING FIRES

PREFACE

"God looked into the letters of the Torah and created the universe," wrote the author of the Zohar, a medieval Jewish text. The author also speculates that the letters are black fire on white fire, radiating life. In related texts throughout centuries, sages have made great claims about the letters' powers: meditating on them can bring one into the divine presence; on uttering certain combinations, one can raise the dead, even create a golem—a human being.

This book is my midrash, my exploration of the twenty-two letters of the Hebrew alphabet—the alef-beit. A midrash is an interpretation of the Torah, especially its many gaps or conundrums. The midrashim of certain rabbis have been preserved as collections of writings, which are part of rabbinical and scholarly tradition. The twenty-two letters became for me doorways into one strand of that tradition—the entangling 2,000-year-old hermeneutic conversation known as the Kabbalah.

The primary source for belief in their magic is the sayings by which an invisible God speaks the world into being, using the immaterial to create the material, as in this most familiar one:

> When God began to create heaven and earth—
> the earth being unformed and void, with darkness
> over the surface of the deep and a wind from God
> sweeping over the water—God said, "Let there be
> light"; and there was light.

The complex network of meanings that have accrued to the letters themselves all relates in some way to their three attributes—their shapes, names, and numbers—and to where and how the letters and the words they constitute appear in the Torah. Similar to some Chinese characters, the shapes of many Hebrew letters resemble forms found in the world, and their names generally relate to that form. For example, *beit,* the second letter of the alef-beit, is shaped like a house (or some say an open tent door), and its name means "house."

Each letter is also a number, which means that Hebrew words can be summed. The method of converting words into numbers and studying their numerical significance is known as gematria. Rabbis and other Torah scholars look for words, phrases, and sentences in the Torah with similar sums and decipher those connections, believing they reveal hidden divine meanings. This practice is also applied to the letters themselves; for example, the shape of the letter *alef* (1) is created by combining two *yud*s (10 + 10), and a *vav* (6). The sum of the letters is 26, the same sum as that for the most sacred name of God, thereby revealing that God is One.

The three sections of every poem in the first two parts of this book correspond to the attributes of the letters: the first relates to its form in the world, the second to its name, and the third to its number. The final three poems contain only the first two sections.

I began writing these poems as a collaboration with Dennis Evans, a remarkable Pacific Northwest visual artist whose mixed-media pieces alchemically layer languages and other signs on painted beeswax canvases and glass vessels. On these swirled burnt surfaces, he affixes imaginary objects that resemble those in the real world, giving his work a reverential yet nonreferential mythological cast.

Together we invented a narrative about an adept's journey that draws from Jewish tradition but that also is rooted in our artistic traditions and work. Our organizing metaphor was the letter seen as a toolkit containing esoteric and artistic knowledge, which, if mastered at each stage of the journey, could lead one to invent a universe. We named each kit so that it corresponded both to a stage and, where possible, to its traditional Jewish meaning. Additionally, for each name Dennis invented a visual symbol, providing an alphabet that viewers and readers can use to perform a kind of gematria.

The poems about the first nine letters tell a linear story, which is obviously and easily related to the Jewish name of each letter. One shoulders the yoke of *alef* and sets out to invent a self. The next nine poems comprise a series of trials rather than a sequential story, and the last four present the insights of a realized adept, realized, that is, within a specific tradition. To underscore that these poems are indebted to and take place within the Jewish tradition, for the final poem of the book I chose to loosely translate an eighth-century midrash on the letter *tav* from the Alef-Beit of Rabbi Akivah.

Writing within our collaborative structure and the Jewish tradition required that I work with a letter for weeks and months until a poem arrived. Whereas religious Jewish thinkers believe the Hebrew alphabet is a code that reveals divine intention, I came to see it as a code that reveals the limits and generative power of language. I studied the letters in the same way I study Zen koans: I absorbed their source texts and interpretations (Torah stories, psalms, poems, paintings, calligraphy), living with them until an experience or insight shattered their language and logic, revealing what they concealed. These poems are my responses, my riveting and my rivulet to a mutable tradition that is continually beginning.

Emily Warn
Spring 2008

SHADOW ARCHITECT

THE YOKE
OF HEAVEN

Alef: THE YOKE OF HEAVEN

The Yoke of Heaven

Shoulder your sack of barley and oats,
your burden lifts as you walk.

No need to know who beckons.
Stir any of God's seventy names

until hummingbirds thrum in your throat.
Skim creeks, honeyed meadows,

then climb a dry plateau to your beginning:
                    a fallow field, unplowed.

Seeding an Alphabet

To invent the alef-beit,
decipher the grammar of crows,
read a tangle of bare branches
with vowels of the last leaves
scrawling their jittery speech
on the sky's pale page.

Choose a beginning.
See what God yields and dirt cedes
when tines disturb fescue, vetch, and sage,
when your hand dips grain from a sack,
scattering it among engraved furrows.

Beyond the hill, a plume of dust
where oxen track the hours.
Does God lead or follow or scout?
To answer, count to one again and again:
a red maple leaf and a yellow maple leaf
that wind rifles and rain shines until they let go,
blazing their scripted nothingness on air.

From the Beginning

Is it to fix memory that you want me to speak? Sit here on
this rocky outcrop and give me your walking stick. Yoked to
each other, we are God's draft animals, a farmer and his
team of oxen turning at the field's edge until a square is
lined. Stop tugging the cart to the right or left. Sink your
feet into axle-deep dust and pull.

God looked into [the letters of] the Torah and
created the universe.

> the Zohar

And He created His universe with three
books, with text, with number, and with
communication.

> *Sefer Yetzirah: The Book of
> Creation,* translated by
> Aryeh Kaplan

Drive your cart and your plow over the bones
    of the dead.

> William Blake, "The Marriage of
> Heaven and Hell"

Beit: THE HOUSE OF MUSING

Dwelling Place

Where two rivers merge among cottonwoods,
where salmon scour mud from bottom stones,

walk along riverbanks scattering seeds.
Find a hollow bone, a riddled snag to siphon sky.

When kingfishers dive for your low notes,
when light rests from storing packets in trees,

steal the blessing for the doorpost.

The House of Musing

The trick? To live without survival kits:
miracles, bottled water, fire starters, spells.

To stop grumbling to God and build
your hut in the wilderness.

No need to search or not search.
Just join hay stalk to hay stalk, bale to bale

until thick walls swathed with mud appear.
From within, the doorway frames the quiet

of a tree with a single leaf. You're safe
to examine the distance you've crossed.

How you lived not knowing you lived.
How you postponed this reckoning

believing you lacked a desire to know.
Yet here you are listening to a leaf

scrape air, your hands smeared with mud.

Tycher Library
7900 Northaven Road
Dallas, TX 75230

The Tent of Meeting

To make two, withdraw into one. Engrave a hiding place
where rabbis and refugees mingle. On the lower level,
hollow out crannies for spare lights and purified water, for
grain, stray cats, and a companion whom you desire as
continuously as you desire the rabbi to sing God's names:
Elokim and Havayah. Then the refugees will gather, pulling
tefillin and siddurim from inside large coats, rocking
and muttering their prayers to the rabbi's *O Hear O Hear
O Here Is One.* Stop scouting from the perimeter. Stop
admiring the vessel you made from your loneliness. The
sputtering cursive of the hearth fire, the unspeakable name!

Creation is an emanation from the divine light;
its secret is not the coming into existence of
something new but the transmutation of the
divine reality into something defined and
limited—into a world.

Adin Steinsaltz, *The Thirteen
Petalled Rose*

In that place I will allow you to speak my Name.

Exodus 20:21

Lord, who may sojourn in Your tent,
who may dwell in Your holy mountain?

Psalms 15:1

Gimel: THE MASTER GARDENER

The Bridge Lesson

Now that you have found me,
you'll learn where to dig for Joseph's bones
and why Moses carried them through
                              wilderness to Canaan.

Their rattle is a pact
to recollect the others, too,
who lugged filched candlesticks
                              and slave memories

without which they would have stayed
mingling with Egyptians
while you mastered the art
                              of preserving the dead.

The Master Gardener

Pull up a chair. Here's how
to breathe life into a woman
who every morning sweeps her porch
clean of dust and spiderwebs,
who waters lilacs planted in memory
of her husband dead for twenty years.

She returns at dusk to wait for spring
when the sun's arc lights purple torches
                    for hummingbirds,
a traveling flock with no preacher,
              her grief their nectar.

She repeats her task to pass the time
building a bridge to the missing.

Now begin.

The Infinity Lesson

God spoke heaven and earth into being, dividing and
joining them with a sound that is no sound. With light,
God struck the number 1 out of formlessness. Counting and
saying begin with this vanishing point, how adding 1 to 1
makes 2, and 1 to 2 makes 3, and so on. The number 3
locates infinity in a room we can never leave; motion is
impossible if space and time can be subdivided infinitely.
Words and numbers prove we are points on a line stretching
from now to when.

The first line of the creation story can be represented in mathematical terms as a natural progression. Nothing precedes zero. Zero represents beginning, God is one, heaven and earth are two, and, as we will see, space is three. Thus, *Ein Sof* precedes and must first create Nothingness before the names of God.

Rabbi David A. Cooper,
God Is a Verb

And why is the gimel's leg extended toward the dalet? The gimel is like a person who sees a poor person at his door who goes into the house to bring out some food for that person.

Otzar Midrashim: Alef-Beit of
Rabbi Akivah

Have I not written you a threefold lore in wise counsel to let you know truly reliable words.

Proverbs 22:20–21

Dalet: THRESHOLD

Threshold

Brick by brick you built
a dwelling place to arrive

where you can set out.
You framed a doorway

with a view of what's outside
and in. Now join the two.

Step through
            the nothing you contain.

Passageway

You are a shadow of a door falling
into the light of its doorway.

Open or closed, you withstand rain,
wind, lights, newspapers, boots, keys.

You echo each beckoning until you hear
what people spoke at the Place of the Pillar

where the vessel of language broke,
dispersing them north, south, east, west.

Its shattering reaches you when conjuring fails.
It is the loneliness of shards and trading posts.

At the markets for winter, spring, summer, fall,
barter stories for tongues of ox and the four primal seeds:

corn, beans, squash, rye. At harvest rub silk blades
on your face. Recite what you receive.

This is the fourth poverty of exaltation.
You are a doorway through which the ancestors walk.

Mezuzot

Doorways are vanished places of the names of ancestors
migrating from one holy place to another. The retelling of a
legend over generations makes it holy. When a stranger
knocks, search the cellar for last year's root crops buried
under sand. Serve the corner piece from the kugel and pour
her a glass of wine. Sing the stranger's name over and over,
until it is the time when angels of death issue instructions
to tornadoes, rain clouds, grasshoppers. Concocting safe
passage through drought is more difficult. A young God
sings open the doorways of the sea. Miriam dances with
her timbrel and tambourine, and we love for weeks on
the beach.

———————

The *dalet* is the door through which the humble enter into the realization of G-d's dwelling place below.

> Rabbi Yitzchak Ginsburgh,
> *The Alef-Beit*

After Spinoza, philosophers know that they are using language to clarify language, like cutters using diamonds to shape other diamonds. Language is seen no longer as a road to a demonstrable truth, but as a spiral or gallery of mirrors bringing the intellect back to its point of departure.

> George Steiner, *Language and Silence*

That stony law I stamp to dust: and scatter
    religion abroad
To the four winds as a torn book, & none shall
    gather the leaves.

> William Blake, "America"

Hei: ELIJAH'S BABBLE

Breaking the Tablets

How safe to listen to God,
to chisel script on granite.

Sparks fly. You assign numbers
to letters; sum words to glean

correspondences, analogies,
binaries, metaphors, keys.

Your face is lit as you descend
until you hear the crowd

praise another man's handiwork.

Elijah's Babble

After my rendition in the cave,
they engraved my name in a pink granite star

on Hollywood Boulevard. People mill about.
I swore fame was someone else's story.

Cameras flash. Some touch my gold letters,
a gravestone in any other setting.

Dizzy and Thelonious said without speaking a word.
Their riffs stopped taxis, got people to tapping

and listening, forgetting their business.
I'm proof that words travel to jazz's galaxy.

Not any words, words that labor where no one speaks.
To hear them, I squandered nights in whiskey bars,

lapped milk that widows left for starving cats,
wandered streets until I could hear what is not;

not the earthquake that sets old clocks and hearts ticking,
not the firestorms that smoked all summer,

not the wind snapping power lines, leaving us in the dark,
but the sound of God almost breathing.

A Short History of Language

The mountains smoked and trembled. The cave shook loose
rocks. Numb and terrified, we assembled broken stones to
mark our assembly place. We charted how hawk cries shatter
air before they dive through. We began to howl, jeer, preach,
plead, ignite before we became ash and bone, bone and ash,
drifting shapes in a cold sky that others might see.

Unlike numbers, words do not contain within
themselves functional operations. Added or divided,
they give only other words or approximations of
their own meaning.

George Steiner, *Language and
Silence*

You will follow the book, whose every page is an
abyss where the wing shines with the name.

Edmund Jabès, *The Book of
Questions,* translated by
Rosemarie Waldrop

They rush to His saying like a whirlwind.

*Sefer Yetzirah: The Book of
Creation,* translated by
Aryeh Kaplan

Vav: THE PARCHED SEEDS

The Parched Seeds

Those words on parchment
rolled inside a wormwood box

have gone dry and flat.
Repeat them day and night

until brittle as fired clay
they chip and break.

Silence sweet as sleep
answers. Then a dog,

a train's whistle, and rain.

Rainmaker

What they can count on are stones,
a couple of creosote bushes, sheep bawling,

bickering children and priests,
blisters, and Miriam dead.

Her kaddish and her days of shiva
chanted, their clothes rent.

They have charred wood,
scouts returning with empty gourds.

No figs, no grain, no pomegranates,
    no vines, and no water.

At dawn, the hills turn pink, glare.
At night, stars hang too close

with no moon, no Miriam.
    Lost radiance.

The people congregate.
They smoke and point

from coal to constellation,
from dying ember to dying ember.

The flying sparks etch *Mother,*
fading to memory on the night sky.

To be on the move with her,
to jettison Moses in the Tent,

memorizing thirty-two paths of wisdom
and fifty gates of understanding.

Whom will they run to, legs flying
over stones and grass? Who will stroke
                              their hair?

Moses beats the rock with his hand—

What do they know?
Miriam watched over me.

He flails his rod against the rock
until a channel opens for his tears.

They weep and he weeps some more,
then they drink and the beasts drink.

Face-to-Face

Miriam arrives at dusk in a desert thunderstorm from a
direction you least expect. You've been walking away from
her, tending your slights. She invites you to look into her
face. The vav of connection is the impossibility of knowing
oneself except in the gaze of another. When your gazes
meet, an insurmountable distance arises and a desire to
diminish it with speech.

My soul clings to the dust.
Revive me in accordance with Your word.

Psalms 119:25

The Israelites arrived in a body at the wilderness of
Zin on the first new moon, and the people stayed
at Kadesh. Miriam died there and was buried
there. The community was without water, and
they joined against Moses and Aaron.

Numbers 20:1–2

Has the Lord spoken only through Moses? Has he
not spoken through us as well?

Numbers 12:2

Zayin: JUBILEE

The Sabbath Queen

She is always flowing through
these flimsy tents of skin and bone.

Knit your soul to hers
as pine needles knit stars.

Tremble when she pulls you close
to read in your eyes a sign.

She mirrors until the mirror disappears
and you know yourself to be in her, of her
worshiping.

Returning Light

You pull a few weeds, mostly dandelions
whose thick roots dive beneath rocks.

They break off. You curse
though there's no sense peppering air

or disturbing pollen waiting for wind
to inflate its yellow cloud and drift.

You dust for prints—she lives here somewhere.
You prowl with your weed buckets and nets,

with your dictionaries and opera glasses.
For company, you have a dying cat

and a rabbi who rides his bicycle up
and down the alley looking straight ahead,

neither picking the blackberries
nor listening to the white Victrolas of morning glories.

Their vines scratch out dumped car seats,
spokes, weed clippings, a gold watch—

clues to keep you digging and sifting.
The dandelions spring back,

the cat dies, the rabbi switches shuls.
She remains, orienting you south.

Jubilee

On the seventh day, gather in the fields, at coffee shops,
hamburger joints, on the beach, in strip-mall parking lots,
city parks, outside liquor stores. Bring old appliances:
toasters, mixmasters, coffee mills, food processors, electric
can openers, ice-cream makers, microwaves. Bring Sears-
guaranteed-for-life screwdrivers, pruning saws, crowbars,
pickaxes, sledgehammers, flat-nosed shovels, steel rakes.
Bring vases of gladioli, asters, penstemons, dahlias,
anemones, coneflowers, pansies. Bring your last pay stub,
diplomas, wedding invitations, bar mitzvah prayer books,
final exams, driver's licenses, dental records. Bring steel-
drum barbecues, Webers, clay chimineas, portable fire pits,
camp stoves, fire bowls, hibachis. Bring milkweed pods,
sycamore mines, rose hips, maple wings, cottonwood fluff,
dandelion propellers, burs. Give them away to neighbors.
Recline on lawn chairs. Play hopscotch with children. Make
yourself a fitting vessel to receive love as smoky barbecue,
love as games, love as repair, love as love, love as petals, love
as telling, love as holy days.

All sevenths are beloved.

VaYikra Rabbah 29:10, Midrash
Rabbah to Leviticus 29:11

They would cook some fish, sell some and buy
with the proceeds wine and go out into the fields
and give their husbands to eat there. After they
had eaten they took their mirrors and looked into
them together with the husbands. She said: I am
more comely than you. He said: I am more
comely than you. In the course of this (tête-à-
tête), their sexual desire was aroused and they
became fruitful and multiplied.

Midrash Tanchumah,
Parshat Pekudei 9

Do not forsake your mother's teaching.
Tie them over your heart always,
Bind them around your throat.

Proverbs 6:20–21

Chet: HOVERING

Wild Rose Agriculture

From brittle twigs,
push pale green stems,
      no toughness.
At their tips—
      cupped pink roses
with bees inside,
      kicking, jiggling,
rubbing pollen all over their bellies.
A wind gust sways the nests.
The bees hold tight to stamens, buzz.
Snubbed, the wind moves off to pick apart seeds.

Hovering

You close your book of proverbs
on a hillside of sweet peas cloudy with bees.
They push apart petals and dive in
until all you see are vibratling stingers.
Five seconds… until they buzz off
to another cluster. Sip and run.
How do they find the sweet spot?
Scent? A shade of pink? Tone?

The pop of seedpods bursting in the heat,
a sparrow singing scales in Queen Anne's lace,
others chirp, chirp   chip.   Chirp chip.
Buzzzzzzzzzzz uzzzzz—chirp   chirp.
You add your moan, your long *oh*
with an *ummm* at the end, reverberating
with the bee tone and a single-engine plane drone
until the world is humming one song
and everything that rises is a riff:
the sparrow bursts from single notes
to a trill, the plane circles, children shout.

Once before you heard this music
and thought such clarity could last.
Now you know that was that state, and this
is a tangle of sweet pea vines and buzz.

You break off a flower. You part the lips.
No sweetness. No nectar. No scent.
This hillside contains all states of flowering,
of manufacturing sweetness and being sucked dry.
The lavender petals turn blue, then dry to brown
then bleach white as skin after death.
On any single vine—rattling pods and blossoms.

Harmony

Chords from symphonic strings, reeds, dried animal hide,
stretched taut over space caught in long cylinders of flutes
and clarinets, in the wide hips of tubas, in the slender
vases of violins. We stroke the guts and skin with bows and
tongues, with fingers and sticks until sound emerges in
pulses, approximating a flurry of bees, which pulse and
vibrate not with their wings but through porous bodies, a
million undetectable openings through which air flows.
What we hear as buzz, what we see as a swarm, a shape
forming and re-forming as it moves through space, is noth-
ing more than a conversation necessary to survival, relaying
the source of food, directions to a clover meadow mixed
with red paintbrush. The paintbrush gives the honey a dis-
tinct taste on our tongues as we dine and talk, complaining
about what we have not yet perfected—the harmonic made
when a wet finger lightly circles a fluted champagne glass,
the tone stopping us from hearing our less-detectable hum.

Take your sandals from your feet
For the ground where you stand is holy.

Joshua 5:15

To forget and blossom, to blossom and forget,
    is all.

        Yehuda Amichai, "Sadness of the
        Eyes and Descriptions of a
        Journey," translated by the author
        and Ted Hughes

I do not snivel that snivel the world over,
That months are vacuums and the ground but
    wallow and filth,
That life is a suck and a sell, and nothing remains
    at the end but threadbare crape and tears.

        Walt Whitman, "Song of Myself"

Tet: HOW THE TWO BECOME ONE

How the Two Become One

Jacob wrestled wind
howling inside him
until it returned
his brother's face,
as when wind shakes the leaves
after a brief summer rain
to prolong its sweetness
and startle the trees
into thinking they're clouds.

Face-to-Face

Alone, I waited
on the riverbank
for you alone,
having sent my sheep
ahead to placate you.
On seeing them,
you ran to meet me.
We embraced, and wept.

Jacob, you've come back at last,
to mend our rift, you said.
For me, it was no more,
except when I clung to the past,
mulling it with grief.
Go on your way, Jacob, you urged
with no reproach, *but keep*
your offering, salted with fear.

A crow woke my old dog
asleep in muddy rushes
beside the riverbank.
It woke me, too.
I listened to the current
dividing me from you,
a ghost the crow scares away.
Then I saw your face
as one might see God's face.
Its kindness, the love
I felt in the womb returned.

Esau, I begged,
accept my gift.
I will, you said,
looking through me,

and wished me safe journey,
refusing my request
to keep step with mine.

Purifying the Vessel

Lie down on the baked earth in a field of dry grass and clover. Coil your walking stick into a snake. Listen to the wind praise the flimsy, disorderly nests of crows, how they fly all day carving tunnels for night to enter. When you hear the wind bend the grasses into letters and sing their shapes, rise and lead the congregation in the study of sea fossils and generations of locusts.

I never could forget you.
See, I have engraved you
On the palms of My hands.

Isaiah 49:15–16

The essential property of the Name is mercy; by emulating G-d's mercy we reveal His Name.

Rabbi Yitzchak Ginsburgh,
The Alef-Beit

According to Kabbalah, the *tet* resembles a snake coiled head into tail.

Rabbi Yitzchak Ginsburgh,
The Alef-Beit

THE SOUL'S
CHISEL

Yud: THE HAND OF GOD

Handiwork

At dawn God opens one hand
to let cramped darkness flee.

All night clouds of glory
float beyond reach of dreams,

beyond a prayer book and a clock,
which wait with you until dawn

to help you wrestle the dark
back into God's other hand.

The Hand of God

They scratched Your Names on wooden slats, in soot,
on paper scraps in Bergen-Belsen, Auschwitz, Babi Yar.

In Warsaw they buried Torahs in rusty milk cans
with keepsake diamonds, eyeglasses, fountain pens.

No rescue arrived, no maps with dotted lines,
no gruel, no clothing, no sheltering dust.

What they possessed were Your Names,
the little that is much, the point of a yud,

a speck of hope that someone would hear
what they had seconds to say

before firing squads whipped wind,
toppled them broken dolls into graves.

First one spoke, then ten, then ten times ten
until a murmuring arose Elokim   Havayah

Adonai   El Shaddai   Hashem
Havayah   Shechinah   Asherah

summoning all the Names where You
were not until all that was or will be

became Elokim, Havayah, Shechinah
gathering outstretched hands to heaven.

The Vanishing Point

You slow down to watch cumulus clouds stream across the
sky. You choose a more circuitous route home and pass a
tree with white bags tied around random apples. The apples
remind you of clouds, how each hangs in the sky, singular
yet part of a flock. Each item in the flock is a coordinate of
earth and sky, enumerating space. The flocks of apples and
clouds are actual infinities, an endless collection of discrete
items that one can conceivably count to the end. This is
different from potential infinity, which is the entirety of
infinity, an immeasurable continuum that is greater than the
sum of its parts. After your first glimpse, you are lonely for
more contraction of space around the light of your mind
contemplating what cannot be conceived. What cannot be
conceived this morning? The Army has found the larynx of
an Iraqi man that American soldiers slowly strangled to
death. His ribs, additional evidence for the trial, are still
missing. They are in a refrigerator in Washington, D.C.
These are discrete items; whereas how the passage of time
felt as the soldiers strangled him is a continuum of infinite
pain. And his words and songs and prayers and curses he
will never speak are an empty set.

My groaning serves as my bread;
My roaring pours forth as water.

Job 3:24

Before the creation of the world, He and His
Name were Alone.

Pirkei d'Rabbi Eliezar

He hid me in the shadow of his hand.

Isaiah 49:2

Kaf: CANTILLATIONS

The Palm of God

Make a vessel for what you cannot grasp,
for the light you siphon from the sky.

Spill it in your palms. Examine its glint.
Blow gently—a milkweed seed from a burst pod—

one breath and it disappears to plant itself…
where? Over there a shoot points

to sun winking in the crown of a palm tree.

The Crown of God

At dusk in drenched, silvery grass,
in the open space of a city park,
you stop walking to better hear
a thunderstorm, now distant, grumbling,
hiking deeper into the Appalachians.

The elms and sycamores lean in,
scooping shadows from the grass,
gathering them into their branches,
crowded, clamoring with cicadas
that gather what's left of light.

You stand on clay feet, wearing the same shoes
Joseph's brothers sold for twenty shekels,
and strain to catch the cicadas handing off
their buckets of sand from tree to tree;
their toneless incessant scraping sifts time for us.
A firefly blinks on at your feet. One star blinks back.

Cicadas praise the trees
            for standing still.

They praise the fireflies,
            lamps for their night's work.

They praise the stars
            for bursting their bounds.

They praise the hoarse oak leaves
            for their ceaseless muttering.

The fireflies are gems
in the crown of God
resting on your head.
Your palm longs to cup

the head of the person you love,
to brush the tips of grasses.
You pluck a few stems
to decorate the brim
of your straw hat.
From horsetail stems
and beetle wings
you fashion a hummingbird
and wrap its wire claws
around a fern, shaped
into a Hawaiian palm
shading a beach
on which you walk
scattering wilted daisies
and gold coins.
You take off your shoes
to lie on your back in the sun.
You notice how the sun
stirs light into the waves,
how it rests its palms
on the beach, on your head.
You fall asleep
while it engraves
the dreams of God
among the myrtle trees
of Amni-nadib.

Cantillations

How do you remain faithful when boredom sets in? Sages offer numerous rules of piety, precepts, commandments, vows, proverbs, and aphorisms, all compiled after revelations that shattered the structure of existence. The purpose of all rules of piety is to extend revelation into ordinary life. They are survival tactics that help us withstand tedium, our disappointed expectations that something dramatic will happen—the sky open, a pillar of fire light our way—if we do this and that. For example, if you stand in a field in the month of Elul when the red dwarf rises above the tree where the shepherd has tethered his goats, you'll see divine light. Instead, you are preoccupied with stamping your feet in the cold, with muttering and gossiping with friends. Without knowing it, you're storing a memory of being knit together that will help you survive later. You'll remember one friend who rolls her eyes in mock disapproval at such religiosity; another concentrates as hard as she can on what the sages said would happen if you gathered in the fields during the month of Elul. She focuses on waiting to see a flash. The other observes what can be seen, the night sky, its billions of unnamed stars, impossible to count, immeasurable depth, formless space, black, blank; receding as she is, less and less visible, less and less impatient at nothing much happening. The other shouts, witnessing the birth of a star.

A remorseful life is a living corpse.

Midrash

Even the illiterate among you are as full of
precepts as a pomegranate.

Berachot 57a

Not to waste time is to contain the passage of
days and months within your skin bag, without
leaking... To waste the passage of time is to be
confused and stained in the floating world of
name and gain. Not to miss the passage of time is
to be in the way for the way.

Dōgen, *Enlightenment Unfolds*

Lamed: OX-HERDING LESSON

Ox Goad

What did you expect? Accolades?
Laurels without thorns? To have come this far…

To have grasped God's hand…
Be wary when your burden lightens.

Your heart is wrestling an ox
in a muddy feedlot with an open gate!

He doesn't move. You prod him with spurs.
He swishes flies, bellows, backs away.

Come on! Get up! Look!
Beyond the gate—a green pond
                  in an untrammeled field.

Ox-Herding Lesson

The road bends away
      from the sea,
           meandering
through salt meadow hay.
You walk along singing
      on the road of white sand
          dug from the marsh,
the sea a hushed roar in the distance
where the forge of waves
         levels the sand,
spilling its molten silver
      at the sandpipers' feet
         that scurry, jotting it all down.

Just ahead of you on the road
is an egret, perfectly still,
      perfectly white
and shaped like a lamed,
the only letter with its top
      in the clouds,
the only letter that leans
    like marsh grass,
one eye cocked on ditch water,
      the other on clouds—
        white feathers,
          aloft yet earthbound.

The egret is dwarfed by salt marsh,
    which stretches far, far
         away,
a wind-flattened white sea of grass

with islands of scraggly myrtles
                              rising
from it. And dwarf cedars whose outer needles burn
                    to protect the living sap.

Egrets can stand so still among reeds
                    that fish mistake their legs for grass.
Why then is this one in the road
              when ditches on either side teem
                              with minnows?

You sit down on hot gravel to ask
                              and hear
the egret listening to you
              pierce and swallow
                              the atmosphere of fishes and clouds.

Psalmistry versus Prophecy

King David preferred composing tunes in minor keys to evoke nostalgia for the divine rather than rousing people. He rejected the prophets' belief in a hierarchy of sages. To ascend the prophetic ranks, David would have had to excel in asceticism, wandering in rags, recording the world's misery and shouting, always shouting to snag people's attention. He dreaded the prophecy Olympics, the competitions for turning one's walking staff into a snake and interpreting animal-husbandry dreams. He wavered, though, when he thought about giving up prophecy's pyrotechnics: igniting incendiary bushes and eternal sparks, salting clouds with light. As a psalmist he could dispense with all that bravado. To court inspiration, he concentrated on moping after the sacred. This required watching olive trees shake down the wind and spying on lovers in blossoming nut groves. On days he couldn't detect longing, he would sink to Sheol. There he'd gather faint light in his palms and tie the thread of a dwindling autumn river around it.

How good is a word rightly timed.

Proverbs 15:23

We of Israel taught that the Poetic Genius (as you
now call it) was the first principle and all the
others merely derivative, which was the cause of
our despising the Priests & Philosophers of other
countries, and prophecying that all Gods would
at last be proved to originate in ours & to be the
tributaries of the Poetic Genius. It was this that
our great poet King David desired so fervently &
invokes so patheticly.

William Blake, "The Marriage of
Heaven and Hell"

The words "kidney-fat of wheat" (Genesis 27:28)
apply to Halakhot [laws], which are the essence of
Torah; and the words "of the blood of the grape
thou drinkest foaming wine" (Genesis 27:28)
apply to Aggadot [legends], which gladden a
person's heart like wine.

Sifrei Parshat Ha' Azinu,
section 12

Mem: THE SOUL'S CHISEL

The Covenant

A tugboat labors,
        pulling a barge
                loaded with sawdust
across the sea,
        sketching
                on the choppy surface
a shiny wavering line.

The Soul's Chisel

A wide brown river swirls through boulders.
Downstream bubbles pop in calmer pools.

You break a stick and toss it in to sweeten the water.
The current herds it past logjams into the flow.

It shivers in a slight disheveling wind
carrying memories of winter.

You hide in a cleft of rock
to watch God pass by.

You could call out God's Name.
You could dazzle God with stories

sung each year when runoff
exposes the oak tree's roots,

except the Dust of the Cloud,
the Shadow, would obscure this opening.

You grow still as the rock,
as obdurate, though mica glints

among lichen blossoms,
though ants trace igneous scars,

though the rock's jagged edge inspired seventy scribes
to impress seventy languages in wet clay.

At the next approach, you hear
that which the river absorbed from the rock,
                    the rock from the river.

The House of Fluency

You trudge to shore and no wave road opens on the surface
sheen of cloud shadows and wings. Behind you, the ox road,
a track to this trackless blue. You lunge through surf until
the bottom drops away. On rolling swells you float between
sky and sea, then dive, threading passageways among coral
boulders, anemone studded. You follow blind fish, find a
violin with missing strings, a glass float, a mouth harp.

Mem is the substance of mother earth. It is water (*mayim*) and it is the wilderness (*midbar*) through which we wander and are made ready.

Lawrence Kushner, *The Book of Letters*

The glory of God is to conceal things.

Proverbs 25:2

There is no water except Torah.

Bava Kama 17a

Nun: THE SHADOW ARCHITECT

The Shadow Architect

He shoulders a portable temple for words,
a holy space with no purpose

other than to house the Name
for what has no measure—

no height, no width, no circumference—
yet is what trues our days.

The Tabernacle

Hope fills me this morning as I fashion letters
into a tree that sighs, that stays put yet moves,
reaching to its limits, swaying and settling,
a compass pointing to its place on earth
where every morning it blocks the sun
for me, at work in my studio,
where I scratch and scrawl and loop
letters into shapes so I can enter the Tabernacle
of their bodies and hear each foot, each syllable
sending its roots to a depth as great as that tree's,
which has been standing and rooting and swaying
long before I came to memorize its plain mystery,
its wide-bodied hull open to stars at night,
each a point that I lengthen into a letter
and each letter into a word, and with the words
build a Tabernacle for the ten most broken
and the ten most resonant words. I will place them
in an inner sanctum enclosed by hanging carpets,
and outside it, another space enclosed by carpets,
and outside it, another, so that those who wish
to read the words, to say them out loud,
must first pull one curtain back and step inside,
and then another, and another until they arrive
in a hushed space, a soundproofed, heavy quiet
where they come to know that which makes all things
                                        day after day,
and out of which the earth was made.
Stepping behind each curtain they learn
that the mystery of making is not a secret hidden within
but a series of moves, a sequence of steps,
outlined on a blueprint with notes and call-outs,
white on black, constellations in the night sky,
the primordial living Torah, circulating in the letters

as trees circulate light, capturing it with their leaves,
caching it within the soil, then drawing it back up,
watering the tallest branches with the radiant dark.

The Shadow Architect's Studio

Here is the sand for tamping out fire, and tongs and fire
pans of gold. On the altar, fragrant incense burns, a blend—
refined, pure, sacred—extracted from resins of gum and
persimmon, mixed with scent of crushed mollusk. Wisps of
smoke filter through a lamp, hammered from one talent of
gold into an almond tree with six branches, and on each
branch, three blossoms. Over there, the rafters from which
Bezalel hung the pendulum moon. Beside it, the charts for
aligning the beams: how many cubits high and wide to mill
the planks, how many cubits tall to cut the acacia poles, set
in sockets of silver, each with a gold hook to hold curtains
woven from linen and wool, then dyed blue with fluid from
Phoenician snails. The curtains separate the ordinary from
the holy, and the holy from the holiest of holies—the Ark
of the Pact. Strange to picture this portable temple for ten
words engraved on stone which claim language is more holy
than image, that Logos precedes cosmos. Yet proof of this
required trading for the finest yarns and most precious
metals, for rare shells and the sturdiest trees, and for the
hours of Bezalel.

Bezalel, the artisan of the Tabernacle, G-d's
"house" during [Israel's] sojourn in the desert,
"knew how to permute letters through which
were created heavens and earth." His name,
Bezalel…, means "in the shadow of G-d."
"To shadow" means "to emulate." So did Bezalel,
through the knowledge of the power of the letters
and their permutations, emulate G-d in the act
of Creation, whose ultimate purpose is that all
Creation become a "house" for G-d.

Rabbi Yitzchak Ginsburgh,
The Alef-Beit

This "likeness" to G-d, similar to that of Bezalel,
refers to [Adam's] ability to "know" reality by
name.

Rabbi Yitzchak Ginsburgh,
The Alef-Beit

You are to make with it something—
Incense,
Perfume of perfumer's making,
Salted, pure—holy.

Exodus 30:35

Samech: THE PERFECT ONE

Processional

The sky unfurls
its monotone gray light
to a smattering
of rain and gold leaves.
A wren sings
the same three notes
as yesterday
when clouds
were peach-colored
roses pinned
to the mountain's
black lapel.

The New Year of the Trees

You watch the sixty queens dance
among snowy pines on Tu Bishvat.

Who lifts their feet? Who swirls
their muslin robes? *Only one is your dove.*

She rests her hand on your hair.
She shines through like the dawn.

For the sake of memory, she whispers,
Dream is one-sixtieth of prophecy.

Their voices rise, a cacophony,
as when wind keens through high surf;

as when tall grass confers its holy orders—
the swaying lanky blue hours.

Your dove could be a concubine, or a maiden,
or you worrying the order of words

will be lost. What if a sickness takes
the damsels without number?

How will you fit long vowel to short,
flat to long, long to long, each in its place,

their places a story about where
they wandered from, or to, or in?

How will you know where to plow a vineyard,
where to sow a patch of sage and myrtle?

One voice rises out of the hubbub,
calls and subsides, calls and subsides.

The Perfect One

What you don't know, that's freedom. Beliefs are mica bits
glittering in dull sand. The sand is the truth, lying there
soaking up the river, or sea, or light. You leave momentary
footprints, impressing yourself. A great sage pressed his foot
into hard granite, and the local people preserved it beside
a temple for centuries. You've seen it and placed your foot
in it. Now you sit by a river watching a flock of cedar
waxwings perform a circus. They snap at insects, stopping
in midflight without falling, mining the air, mining
emptiness for a morsel.

What did the daughters of Israel do? They would
go down to draw water from the river.
Whereupon the Holy One, Blessed be He,
prepared small fishes for them inside their jars.

Midrash Tanchumah,
Parshat Pekudei 9

The sixty tractates are the secrets of the "sixty
queens" (souls of Israel) of the Song of Songs.

Rabbi Yitzchak Ginsburgh,
The Alef-Beit

In *halachah* we find the concept of "nullification
in sixty"..., the quantitative ratio of "disappear-
ance"... or nullification... of one substance...
in another. This is hinted at in [the numerical
equivalent of] the very word for "nothing,"
[ayin]: one [alef] to sixty [samech]. This ratio
appears often in relation to worldly as well as
to spiritual phenomena: "sleep is one-sixtieth of
death"; "dream is one-sixtieth of prophecy"; "fire
is one-sixtieth of hell"; "honey is one-sixtieth
of manna"; "Shabbat is one-sixtieth of the World
to Come."

Rabbi Yitzchak Ginsburgh,
The Alef-Beit

Ayin: PRIME VIEW

Prime View

We prize a view
to steady us.

The mountain range,
our inward quiet.

Cloud shadows
on high glaciers,

our seeking stilled.

Spring Midrash

For no man shall see Me and live...
and My face shall not be seen.
                              (Exodus 33:20)

Then who is it you saw,
or what, sweetening the air?
Not the single white cloud
behind a hill of bare elms,
not the cloud splattered on the river,
not the undulating trunks,
not the wind-broken blue,
but their blend, a current
flowing between mud banks,
our shutters locked open.

    And she lifted up her eyes and she saw.

No leaves yet to stop light from hurtling through.
The creek carries it on its back.
The forest floor stares, starry eyed
with white violets and bluebells,
with bloodroot and bleeding heart.
No heat. No mosquitoes. Just a few gnats
warming up, sugaring the breeze.

    To see is to contemplate a thing until it is understood.
                              (Moses Maimonides,
                                The Guide for the Perplexed)

The spring is too much.
When it gets going sweet gums, redbuds, dogwoods
spatter winter goodbye with mauve smudges,
with lime-yellow simmerings, with white-hot spots
rolling up the hills to fire the leafless trees.

When the day blows gently
and the shadows flee,
set out, my beloved…
for the hill of spices!

(Song of Songs 2:17)

No trail signs until Thompson's Shelter
just as rain scatters campfire ash,
flecks the creek, a storm's slow beginning.

To see not as a subject but as subject to seeing.
What do you see? Branches firing into a pool:
pop, pop, splash. White sparks. Rain flints.
To be always looking for You, eyes cast up
scanning the gray sky held in bony sycamores,
eyes cast down noting rain pocking the creek,
modulating its rush as you rush up the mountain
looking for Your seventy faces.

See I set before you this day ticks and honey,
choose honey.

Each second seventy drops of rain tip the creek;
the rain collects and falls from mountain bowl
to creek, from creek to creek to river, from river to river
to the wide-open pupil of the sightless sea.

Who is watching the creek make its way
over moss, over slick granite slabs, over gravel?
You are watching the creek, you are watching the rain
rivet pools with quick white-hot jabs.

I had heard you with my ears
But now I see you with my eyes.
Therefore I recant and relent.

(Job 42:5–6)

The seventy faces of God are seventy drops of rain
falling each second into the pool.
They are the River Dipper on a rock,
bobbing seventy times before sipping a beakful,
before bathing in the cold oxygen rush.
Each bow, each drop unveils what cannot be seen.

Each second rain pocks the creek, each pock
radiates a circle, a radiant circle, a moon,
a samech, a silver bowl, a yarmulke, an egg,
an esrog, a wedding ring, a pool.

Look into the pool until your eyes are its mirror.
Look until your hair is wet as leaves,
look until your bones are stiff as branches without leaves.
Look until you stop looking and see
rain pocks, ripples, sky splatter, your sighting
here then there moving downstream.

Rules of Piety

Set all your clocks to chime when you can distinguish the
blue from the white weave in your prayer shawl. Remember
not that each second might be your last but that each second
splashes light. Capture it! Capture it!

Do not wait for great enlightenment, as great
enlightenment is the tea and rice of daily activity.

Dōgen, *Enlightenment Unfolds*

The eye never has enough of seeing.

Ecclesiastes 1:8

"Light" (Esther 8:16)—this is Torah.

Babylonian Talmud, Megillah 16b

Pei: INGATHERING OF
THE EXILES

Homeland

The prophets pound on your chest:
Sing. Scrape together notes.

How can I sing when the sea sings?
When boats score the blue?

When wind conducts the clouds
to harbor masts keeping time?

Which words orchestrate
a universe for crying out?

Ingathering of the Exiles

To be no longer wandering,
roast a yearling with bitter herbs

or a goat or a sheep without blemish.
Do not break a bone of it.

Set the table with fine linens,
with two kinds of forks and spoons,

with water glasses and wineglasses,
with silver bowls for peeled eggs.

Fill them four times, even for the children,
even for migraine sufferers and alcoholic poor

who line up on third Tuesdays at St. Vincent's.
Taste the crushed grape and say:

I will free. I will deliver.
I will redeem. I will take.

This is a fixed time and a fixed story.
Drink until your voices blur.

Then and now as it is commanded:
thank, praise, laud, glorify, extol, adore,

not God but the sayings of the Name,
the pei giving voice to the alef,

the story giving voice to us—
chips of light from a shattered source.

Just as rock flints creek water.
Just as, seeing it, one hears

fleeting cloud shadows
illuminating each stretch

so waves of generations of sayings,
of wine light create a ripple effect.

To be no longer wandering,
we debate the nature of unleavened bread.

Which five types of fermented grain
are prohibited to taste?

Wheat barley oats rye spelt.

We dip parsley twice into salt water;
break matzoh, eat horseradish—

white, pulpy, and fiery—until tears well,
a smidgen of the slave's suffering,

then and now, our ancestors and not
our ancestors whom we remember.

For these we relinquish fermented grain.
For these we sling our scythes,

carrying our seed bags, weeping
to replenish the watercourses.

To be no longer wandering,
we open the synagogue's front door.

We turn out the lights and stand up
and sing Elijah's name.

"Is he here?" we ask the children.
And they shout, "Yes, yes!"

above the hubbub of our wine-drinking party,
the servers circling with platters of chicken,

the children dashing under tables
searching for the afikomen,

the parents beaming that their children
will remember what they remember,

as the rabbi works the crowd in his Middle Eastern robes,
saying hello to the Schewells and Cohens and Levys.

We pour him a glass of smuggled Smoking Loon
then go on kibitzing and eating and mingling.

Vows

Praise what you receive. The clack of beetle wings in dry August heat confirms that you are what is continuously given. Listen to midrashim of the rattling crow and the great debates of the chickadees and to the homeless poor, asking for a response as generous as their begging.

The incomparable feature of human language is
that its magical community with things is
immaterial and purely mental, and the symbol
of this is sound.

> Walter Benjamin, "On Language
> as Such and on the Language
> of Man"

Forgetfulness is exile. Remembrance is
redemption.

> Baal Shem Tov (Master of the
> Good Name)

For you will have pact with the rocks in the field.

> Job 5:23

Tzadik: THE SOUL REPAIR KIT

The Soul Repair Kit

You sharpen your stylus and wait
in a tangle of willow and osier.

The river floods you with its names:
flycatchers flutter in the fluttering aspen;

grasses impress shadowy tzadiks on stones.
With spittle, gravel flakes, and mud,

you assemble broken letters in the sandy margin,
repeating their instructions until you are ignorant

as grass, as nameless, seated in the front row
of leaf clappers, chirps, drizzle, and dazzle.

Renewing the Ashen Scriptures

You brush leaves from a stranger
sleeping beside your gate

and welcome him to your estate,
with its sunny fields and barns.

He admires your bins of wing nuts,
your fine linens and deep well.

You show off your net strung between trees
for capturing sunlight, your ponds and goldfish.

In the storeroom, you offer him dates and grain,
purified water, buckwheat, and dry ginger.

Take what you need. Rest.
The stranger answers: *Follow me.*

*I will show you where the trail begins
to the encampment of souls in the forest.*

You follow him across muddy fields,
past the ox swishing its tail, tethered to a tree,

past the pond where stocked fish peer through surface clouds.
At the forest edge, you push through brambles and ivy.

You stuff your ears with moss to mute the abacus of trees
and press through spindly pines into thick woods.

Everywhere God goads you with green ignorance.
The souls of trees shout, *Speak! Speak!*

One of the moon's thirty names will save you.
You forget your hunger, the Names of God, the alef-beit.

God's Withdrawal (Tzimtzum)

When God began to create, He engraved the first letter of
His Name on the Void, then all letters of all His Names, the
first scribe pressing a reed into wet clay. The letters hollowed
a finite space where God wasn't, creating a place for us to be
within the infinite. Sparks, droplets of God remained.
Pollen and dust clung to them becoming hard shells. Sages
polish them until they glint with inklings.

—————————

The final end of knowledge is not to know.

Bechinat Olam 13:45

Be careful in your work, for your work is the
work of Heaven. Should you omit a single letter,
or add an extra letter, you may find yourself
destroying the entire world, all of it.

Sotah 20a Gemara

I was with you when for My Name's sake you
willingly consented to enter the open fire.

Midrash Rabbah to Genesis 39:8

INSTRUCTION FOR LIGHTING FIRES

Kuf: MNEMONIC

1 (*alef*)	Which word struck the first number out of the formless void?
2 (*beit*)	Where do wind and light soap off together in the rain?
3 (*gimel*)	How do you count from zero to one?
4 (*dalet*)	Is there an instant between life and death?
5 (*hei*)	Do the interiors of clouds have moons and planets?
6 (*vav*)	When your shovel scrapes the moonlight on the water, do you stop digging?
7 (*zayin*)	How do coyotes, hunters, and angels mark their principalities?
8 (*chet*)	How do you mingle persimmons and prayers?
9 (*tet*)	Why pour light into a cracked vessel?
10 (*yud*)	Why illumine nothingness then withdraw?
20 (*kaf*)	How does the present tense withstand the nearness of God?
30 (*lamed*)	Who taught language to steal time?
40 (*mem*)	Why do church spires, radio antennas, skyscrapers fish in air?
50 (*nun*)	What is the Name for what has no measure?

60 (*samech*) Who is your dove, your perfect one?

70 (*ayin*) See, I have set before you this day ticks and honey.

80 (*pei*) Whoever writes down the Torah burns it.

90 (*tzadik*) What does a framed pedigree purchase in a forest with no mushrooms?

100 (*kuf*) Does God lead or follow or scout?

200 (*reish*) To find the square root of holiness, totter around thieves.

300 (*shin*) Is the invisible light at the base of a candle flame a throne or a hovel?

400 (*tav*) Why are we born and why do we die with our hands open?

Reish: GENESIS

Genesis

You began without letter or number,
without name or sign, yet you began.

You shouldered, sweated, welded an alphabet,
a horizon kit with chalk to sketch

the line between earth and sky,
to shade in chariots of clouds and fish.

With sheet music and a divining rod,
you sight-read staves and keys,

you spoke in rapid, shallow breaths,
a flame reading the braille of a glowing coal

until you discerned its invisible forge.

Genesis

You hear it in the bird that wakes you at four a.m.,
that sings in response to something you can't see,
can't touch or smell, yet sense in an interval,
which is not exact because you've timed it.
The bird is listening and responding
but to what? To answer, you polish
a stone mirror, you count an abacus of sand.
You pick off Miriam's white scales.
The book of rain writes itself into your will
until you know God is a diva who desires.
She bequeaths you a tin roof for the rainy season.
Each drop, each letter is a beginning,
a startling into speech. Its flash quelling,
for a moment, an inner gabbiness,
a continual boring answer to why, what, how;
can you manufacture light as noiselessly
as ponderosa pines, as stunningly as the ascent
of Calliope hummingbirds that wait
among green ovals of cottonwood leaves,
no larger than half a cigar, iridescent as tree beetles?
These nectar-seeking, oscillating, winged beings
defy your classifying them by size, color, and shape.
Is your impulse to name innate or inherited?
Is wrestling inchoate matter into form love?
If it is, whom are you loving? God? Nature?
Nothingness? Or the mind—that off-kilter,
wobbling gyroscope, incessantly filling nothingness,
which exists only for some things to reflect
each other. Then does nothingness exist?

To memorize the nothing of one river bend,
you walked upstream, balancing on slick stones,
rushing forward, propelled by a desire

to collect impressions, indistinguishable
moments that we are too poorly designed to register.
Our flimsy wiring, our dull mirrors, intended
to help us survive, to block out a stream of sensation,
and yet it is possible to sit still and collect
shades of blue-green in pools beneath willows.
A farther bend is more nearly green,
the impenetrable green of a willow-osier understory
which thrives in the wide, braided, undulant channel,
pouring its hushed showy oratory all day all night
declaring what? The psalmists argue that it's God's handiwork;
the scientists that it's each side of the brain translating;
the rabbis that it's the faint echo of the ten utterances;
the poets that it's the unsaid, the unfinished, waiting
to be expressed, wave after wave, bug after bug
hovering above the surface, jiggling
in electrified, atomized air, in reflected river light,
flames licking the bleached grasses on the riverbank,
dying and fiery in the August heat.

Shin: INSTRUCTION FOR
LIGHTING FIRES

O My Soul

I forged you with my speech.
No longer bereft, you blaze.

The futility of deciphering you—
spark, seed, script, star.

I am yours and you are mine.
No words describe you.

I burn each one so you can see
        within the walls.

Instruction for Lighting Fires

Dry oak leaves, three crossed sticks, and a match.
You fight to kindle it with your breath.

When damp wood sputters and flares,
you doze on branches piled near shore.

Flickering wakes you at midnight.
To lean beyond the circle of light

and puzzle how galaxies and coals—
fitful, appearing and disappearing—

signal each other in the dark.
Leaves rattle and stir, waves sigh,

erasing the border between dreams and fire.
When dawn smudges in the shapes of trees,

the loons talk, the wind murmurs,
illuminating your way home.

Tav: PROPHECY

(The letter tav *from the Alef-Beit of Rabbi Akivah,*
translated by Rabbi Tom Gutherz and Emily Warn)

The Seal

Do not read tav as in "sign,"
the marks of script on parchment;
but rather read ta'avah as "desire,"
the desire of all flesh and blood
every day for all things in this world.
And not only this; even our souls crave,
as scripture says:

> *My soul is consumed with desire*
> *For your rules at all times.*
>
> (Psalms 119:20)

Yet to know these rules is to die and depart,
which is why Job cursed the day he was born,

> *For then I would be lying in repose.*
> *Asleep and at rest.*
>
> (Job 3:13)

For on this earth there is no satisfaction
except a little that a person might live.

Prophecy

See how the human being comes forth
naked from the mother's womb,
without clothes, without covering,
without shoes, without sandals,
without a belt, without a coat,
without thought, without words,
without speech, without advice,
without vindication, without answers,
without strength, without achievements,
without charity, without loving-kindness,
without a husband, without songs,
without a house, without fields,
without vineyards, without gold,
without greatness, without pride,
without everything that God has created.

And when a human being comes forth,
hands open and grasping, she longs
for what cannot be had in this world,
yet she cobbles together an answer
and desires to make something with it,
and develops skill and acquires silver
and fields and vineyards and glory
and honor and everything else God has created here.

Yet when she gains all these things,
she dies and departs from this world
and goes away empty, as it is written.

No matter whether one is a pauper or king,
the moment of death is the same:

> *No man rules the life breath.*
> (Ecclesiastes 8:8)

Then why do we toil *as surely as sparks*
fly upward to fill our mouths when
our appetites can never be sated?

Because it also says,

> *I have placed words in your mouth,*
> *and sheltered you with My hand.*
>
> (Isaiah 51:16)

This means that though our destiny is to die,
we can stand before death happy to have labored
in the Name, as it is written.

ABOUT THE AUTHOR

Emily Warn is the author of two previous books of poems available from Copper Canyon Press. She grew up in Michigan and was educated at Kalamazoo College, the University of Washington, and Stanford University. Her essays and poems appear in *Poetry, Parabola, The Seattle Times, The Kenyon Review, Blackbird, Bookforum, The Bloomsbury Review,* and *The Writer's Almanac.* She lives in Seattle and Chicago, where she is the Webby Award–winning editor for PoetryFoundation.org.

The Chinese character for poetry is made up of two parts: "word" and "temple." It also serves as pressmark for Copper Canyon Press.

Since 1972, Copper Canyon Press has fostered the work of emerging, established, and world-renowned poets for an expanding audience. The Press thrives with the generous patronage of readers, writers, booksellers, librarians, teachers, students, and funders—everyone who shares the belief that poetry is vital to language and living.

Major funding has been provided by:
Anonymous (2)
Beroz Ferrell & The Point, LLC
Lannan Foundation
National Endowment for the Arts
Cynthia Lovelace Sears and Frank Buxton
Washington State Arts Commission

For information and catalogs:
COPPER CANYON PRESS
Post Office Box 271
Port Townsend, Washington 98368
360-385-4925
www.coppercanyonpress.org

The text of this book is set in Adobe Garamond, designed
by Robert Slimbach for Adobe Systems in 1989, based on
the designs of Claude Garamond. Titles are set in Trajan,
designed in 1988 by Carol Twombly, also for Adobe Systems,
based on the letterforms used for the inscription at the base
of Trajan's Column. Book design and composition by Phil
Kovacevich. Printed on archival-quality paper at
McNaughton & Gunn, Inc.

DATE DUE

Tycher Library
7900 Northaven Road
Dallas, TX 75230

3JED000009193S